My HANDICAPPED LIFE

NAVAID HASSAN KHAN

BlueRose ONE
Stories Matter
New Delhi • London

BLUEROSE PUBLISHERS
India | U.K.

For permissions requests or inquiries regarding this publication, please contact:

BLUEROSE PUBLISHERS
www.BlueRoseONE.com
info@bluerosepublishers.com
+91 8882 898 898
+4407342408967

ISBN: 978-93-7139-344-7

Cover Design: Aman Sharma
Typesetting: Manisha Rawat

First Edition: October 2025

Contents

Chapter 1: Introduction

This is pathetic story began with the wedding bells of my dad and mom on 16th oct 1975 where my paternal grandfather who was retired from the army as a Subedar major, He fought in a IInd world war from 1940-45 tied his son's knot with my mom whose father was first Peshkar and later transferred to Raza Degree P.G. College as a Chief Liabrianian. Both families were respectable in Rampur.

My father worked as a Public Relation officer in Raza Textile Ltd. and my mom was a Lecturer of History in N.M.G.I.C, Rampur. Both were happy together in their new life when my mom realized that a third member i.e me was breathing inside her. That was the happiest moment for my parents when on 15th of Aug. I opened my eyes in this big and cruel world and this world became ugliest for me when my parents and I realized that I was not a normal child or should I say a handicapped child, suffering from cerebral palsy (C.P). I started to grow with my abnormalities along with my little sister who came in our life on 26th Jan 1979 that was really a moment of relief for my parents as she was really active like any other normal child.

I have one paternal uncle and two aunties and three maternal uncles and two aunties.

In 1980, I got admission in La Montessori, we studied there till 1988. Then in 1988, we got admission in Greenwood Senior Secondary School and I did my Xth Class in 1993, then I dropped out for one year. My sister got admission in St. Mary's school in 1989 and did her Xth grade from there. In 1994, We both got admission again in Greenwood senior secondary and my sister completed her X11 in 1996 but I came with an incomplete F.sc. Then I completed my I.com in 1997. After that I got admission in a degree college and completed my B.com in 2002. In 2002, I got admission in international ticketing at Sita academy and completed that course in a span of six months. Later, I did my M.B.A from AAIDU 2004 -2006.

Since 2002, till date I am trying for my job according to my profile. I got jobs in Delhi but They were not related to travel sector. I also went to dubai for a job in accounts but I came back on 12th July. I left all my jobs because of my humiliation and in later chapters readers are going to decide how far I am correct. All of them are thinking that I am mentally retarded.

My parents always had confidence in me but now I feel that most of the time, they think about me and taking the chances for the betterment. They talked to one of my aunts for migration to U.S.A especially for me in 1991 but it was not matured. My mother also wrote to one of her colleagues' daughters to U.K., Who gave a positive reply but she missed that fire.

I made a call to one of my uncles for the job, and within a short span he called me back with my appointment in Indian

Islamic Cultural Center (IICC) but within 15 days I left that job because of humiliation by my immediate boss in his own way. On that day I made the decision that I will not return to Delhi for job again.

From that day onwards, I decided not to go back to Delhi until I got a job on my own terms without any humiliation and to be treated like a normal human being. I made up my mind to write about my life experiences and humiliations for those handicapped children and their parents. They will take lessons from my article that, how my parents and I suffered in this ruthless society. I also request all such children not to repeat the same mistakes which I did in my frustration.

Chapter 2:
1977- 1988

My birth on Aug.15, 1977 started a new season in my parents' life. My father was working in a private company "RAZA TEXTILES LTD" and my mother was working as a History Teacher in a semi- Govt. school named NEHRU GIRLS MUNICIPAL INTER COLLEGE (N.M.G.I.C).

In '88 we and our cousins left school. When M. Irfan Lateef sb. came with 4 T. Cs and told us that all the teachers were weeping in the staff room. So, in this way we joined Greenwood SR. Secondary school.

After some days, he left tuition also. In '89 my two cousins went to Bareilly and my sister took admission in St. Mary's. My one cousin and I studied in Greenwood.

My father completed his graduation from Raza Post Graduate college in 1967. He spent 19 years with H.E Murtaza Ali Khan in politics but in vain, then his sister Rajkumari Indra Mohini insisted him to join the company. My mother completed her B.A from the same college and then worked there for a year. After one year, her father sent her to Aligarh Muslim university (A.M.U) for B.Ed. After coming back, she joined the same college. She got lecturership of history in 1986 from L.T Grade giving her precious time to college from 1962.

When I came into this world my father got promoted and gave all the credit to me as he believed, I was lucky for him but my maternal grandmother noticed my activities. I was slow in comparison to other children, I even walked and spoke late. My parents consulted to the renowned ortho. Dr Mini Goyal who then used to work in a handicapped hospital, He analysed me in every possible manner, and made me walk and also suggested my parents to bring me up in a normal environment.

So, my parents admitted me to La Montessori school in 1980. For 15 days, I sat with my principal in her office and when my mother came to take my report she told her that I sit with her in her office. After 15 days I said to her that I wanted to sit in my class with my friends. After the final exams and with a good percentage I was promoted to S. nursery. I was gradually promoted with good division and ranks till the end of VIth std. I wept at home every year that I was not getting 1st rank. In 1987 I got 1st rank in my class in my Vth std. I also stood IInd in school and I got a prize as well; I was very happy.

This is a branch of La Montessori which is owned by Mr. S.N. Bhatla and Raza textile took Rampur branch which is managed by wife of company's joint M. D. Her child was also studied with me. Later he went to school at Dehradun. He is my childhood friend. This school had a healthy atmosphere. The teachers in this school were mostly officers' wives and daughters. Teachers never neglected me and putting me participate in every activity. On my first Annual function fancy dress competition was held and every student got different roles such as toffee, bride, groom, arab billa billa and I was given the role of Nawab sahib. Every student had to recite one poem, but when I finished, my teacher called me down the stage but I recited all the poems of the book. Audience laughed and applaud for me. Teachers used to make me participate in every activity so that I felt I am normal. When I came in higher classes I also played cricket with my friends, my games teacher didn't demoralise me. I performed in every annual function.

In higher classes, my mummy was busy so she said to her sister to arrange a good teacher for my sister and me. My aunt worked in a public library. She arranged one teacher for us who also belonged to a respectable family. He came and taught us until 1988. Later he joined our school. Our performance was very satisfactory in his tenure. He was M.A in English from Raza P.G College. He prepared us for our exams much before in a wonderful manner. He organised my studies in an orderly manner.

I am also a big fan of my English teacher. In a nutshell, the entire staff had a good moral character. They knew how to handle a handicapped child. Later our school's name had changed to Stepping Stones when I was in my 5th or 6th std.

Now, when I failed in every step, I realized and analyzed all amenities of that school. There was a company club, children went there once or twice a year. I watched the movie *Duniya* starring Dilip sb, Rishi Kapoor, Amrita Singh and Jungle book in that club on V.C.R the Teachers and students enjoyed there along with refreshments. The club had wooden flooring. My father told that occasionally officers went there in the evening from the office and played different games. My father mostly played badminton.

Since my childhood, I used to stay at my maternal Grandma's house because my mother was at school. Then from admission, I stayed for almost two years because my bus came there. My both paternal aunties married in Bareilly. After the death of my grandfather my younger aunty came to Rampur, when her son also got admission in our school, the bus started coming to our house. Then I came to my grandma's house. When my bus came there and I was residing at my maternal home so my mother had to go very early in the morning for my bus. When bus came at my residence, So I stayed at my home from 1982 my sister also got admission there.

In upper classes I faced some difficulties in drawing, craft and I took time in copying from the blackboards especially I took entire day in writing the composition of Hindi and English from the copies of my classmates and my handwriting was so bad, but our teachers gave extra time in other periods to complete my essays. My teachers were so kind and caring. They also helped me in my drawing and craft. I salute to the students, staff members and principal who hide my handicappedness in a beautiful manner that I didn't notice it. I was also given extra time during exams. My sister was two years younger, when she grew up, my little sister helped me in every way along with my parents. I had difficulty on buttoning my blue shirts but she would quickly button it up for me. She polished my shoes. In the morning, my mother prepared me lunch boxes and breakfast. So, in the meantime my father and sister helped me to get dressed. My father, mother and my maternal grandma, uncle and aunties held me side by side.

Now I realized I wanted crèches at every time and I got it. At that time my maternal uncle and auntieswere unmarried. My later part of my life which I disclosed later was so bad till date even I recovered it in 1988 in comparison to 1980.

Till 1988 I didn't notice that I was handicapped because of my surroundings.

My father gave his resignation in 1988, so, we all were admitted to Greenwood senior secondary school. I missed the hand of my old school in everyway. I would even daresay, I had said good bye to my luck. I didn't meet a few people from those whom I wanted to meet. If GOD wills, I will one day gather the entire staff and my classmates of my old school yet my memories are still in the rooms of Stepping stones.

Chapter 3: 1988-89

We two along with my three cousins one of which came from Bareilly., after the death of his father . I went to V11 std. I went to Greenwood with the concept that I will get same the atmosphere which I got in Stepping Stones but I was wrong. I came to know immediately that I was handicapped and this was initiated from my residence. when Dr. Alok singhal came to see my grandmother, he saw me and said to my father "This is your child, what happened to him." I was just shocked and came to my mother, my parents gave me courage.

Firstly, I was disturbed that I left the school then I started facing new problems. On the eve of Independence Day, I went to my principal and requested that I wanted to present a speech on 15th August. she replied me, "how will you speak in front of a gathering?", I tried to convince her but she said "No" so. I wept. When she came to know, she allowed me to present the speech but I decided in my heart that I will never participate in any activity of this school. Now, I recall, my humiliation started from the day when I stepped in to Greenwood. My games teacher also did not give me permission to play cricket. I somehow managed my studies, not in a very orderly manner but however I went to the next std. with my normal percentage.

The changes took place in my personal life as well. Firstly, my tutor told to my parents that I will not be able to cope up with Math and Science. He convinced my parents that he didn't has science background and he will arrange a good teacher for me. He arranged a teacher for me in September 1988, and that teacher came. Although He had a science background but he couldn't keep my studies in manner.

My cousin who recently came from Barielly brought some new things in our life for e.g He asked his maternal uncle who lived in AL-Ain ,ABU Dhabi, U.A.E to bring V.C.R and colour t.v so he bought for him .My life changed from two weekly chitarhar, daily soaps and Sunday Evening movie on Black and white t.v to every time movies on v.c.r . The Movies which had a tremendous impact on my life were *Qayamat se Qayamat tak and Maine pyar Kiya.*

I made a friend who also joined school with me. He told me vulgar things; I enjoyed talking with him. Our school went for a picnic to Haridwar and Rishikesh, my cousin asked for him and me. My father refused me because I couldn't manage some certain personal things but he told me later, that my father refused me because I was weak.

In Nov. 1988 we went to my father's friend's daughter's marriage We stood where the food was being prepared. One man said for me in a way why light is shaking and, in another marriage, my elder aunt's younger son told me that I shouldn't hold big bowls as they may break.

In final exams I passed with a second division and I went to VIIIth std. In 1988, I realized that I am handicapped, I couldn't do certain things but I tried, which a normal child of my age could do normally but I failed. I didn't compromise till later years, that I am handy. Now I felt that I wanted to flow against the stream of water which is not possible in any way.

In final exams we passed with second class percentage and I promoted in 8th std.

Chapter 4: 1989 -90

This was the last memorable year of my life which I will never forget it until my death and I wish that from this moment my life to be spent like that.

I counted those years were the best for me in which my performance in studies was well and 1989 was the last good year for my studies. This year was good for me in every way. My younger aunty went to Bareilly, we missed her children but still one cousin remained with me.

My studies began in April '89 and then my summer vacations started. Then In July end, I had my first term exam, I passed every subject but I had less marks in social science but as a result of that I worked hard in it along with other subjects as well. I got a first division in my half yearly exams.

After my first term, one new teacher joined our school and she taught me social science (history, civics and geography). she taught and wrote small notes of the subject on the blackboard; We the students noted it and wrote answers at home. After that class I didn't get this type of notes till end of my studies.

In 1989, both general and state legislative elections were held and Mr. V.P. Singh and Mr. Mulayam Singh Yadav became the Prime minister and Chief minister of U.P respectively.

Chandni was released in October directed by Yash Chopra who is better known for shooting the movie in Delhi and Switzerland, which is the playground of Europe. In this movie Mr. Vinod Khanna played a role of a travel agent. Miss Sridevi worked in his travel agency. Of course, Mr. Rishi Kapoor played a key role in this movie, I liked his dressing sense in the entire film industry.

When I watched this movie, I didn't know, I would choose this profession after completing my studies. When I entirely understand this profession. I went to see the movie to look at the scenes of travel agency. The office was decorated with calendar of airlines and Clock of Lufthansa with a logo. I saw it originally in 2002, the airlines and travel agencies with a big aircraft standing at a gate of the offices.

In feb.1990, the bell rang of my door and I opened the door. The dear fellow asked me about my father and he welcomed him in a nice way. He is Mr. Azhar Inayati, who is a very well-known Urdu poet. I met him then for the first time. He presented his book to my father after writing some note on it. I admire him till now, we often meet and I remember my first meeting at end of my VIIIth std. He also said that he was going to the U.S.A for his Mushaira. I also looked at his Mushira in Dubai, U.A.E which was held in honour of Mr. Jaun Elia , of Amroha(U.P)

My final exams were held and I passed with good marks and went to IX class. I went to classroom some years back and sat on my seat. I wrote some memorable notes on the blackboard. I spent quite a long time alone in this class.

Chapter 5:
1990 -2002

My real humiliation begun in 1Xth std. and there were some faults from my side. My cousin who came from bly. Completed his Xth std in 1990. when I was in VIII std. I heard his activities in the evening at Tea which he did in his class, so I started those types of activities like friendship etc at starting of 1X class.

In 1990, my parents purchased colour t.v and v.c.p when my sister and me insisted them. My cousin went to Bly. But he came back to Rampur with my uncle and took admission in XI and he completed his XII std. in '92 from Raza inter college.

My session begun in April 1990, It was a nice start but later it turned into my failure. When the school reopened in July, Most of my classmates came from cycle and some of them showed me keys of their cycles. I came and requested my parents to buy a cycle for me, but they didn't permit me because I was weak. I was very upset becoz my cousins took the ride of the city. I was not jealous but I wanted to lead a normal life. In the class, teachers were dictated the notes but I was not able to note it down and when I asked my classmates to give me the copy, sometimes they would give and sometimes they wouldn't, because they had to learn. This was the entire year scene. One teacher took three classes of Math, Physics & chemistry. He taught formally in the class and give notes without explaining. He wanted all the students to come to his house to take tution but I didn't go to tution so he ignorned me in the class. My mother sent me from Rikshaw but They were relatives and there was a bitter relationship between us. Due to this he had a bad behaviour towards me. Everybody thought I am mentally weak but it was wrong, for checking him, I used to question him abruptly, but he could never give me any reply and in this way entire year passed.

I didn't have any notes so what I will study at home hence in evening time we were busy in listening hindi songs and sitting Upstairs but I was very worried about my studies.

The system of C.B.S.E also chaged that for passing every student have to take 120 marks to go into new class. There was no question for me to go into X class but the management had decided for those students who didn't do well to dropped them in Boards exams instead of stopping in IXth class. So, I was promoted miserbly to Xth std in 1991. I asked the teachers why they didn't put carbon paper in copies of other students so that I easily got notes of every subject.

In Feb.1991 my grandmother had a fracture so my parents were busy in her.

1991-92: In April my session of Xth Class had begun and same story began in this session as well. The new games teacher also joined and he humiliated me in his own way. In comparison to IX std I felt easy but unfortunately my tutor & I didn't manage my studies properly and I dropped for the first time in my life. I wept so much keeping the head on lap of my mother. In my previous years I felt so bad talking with failure. From my child hood I have bad impression about these students in my mind. I didn't express in words How my heart was broken?

At home the same routine was going on watching released films like *Saajan , Phool aur kante, Sadak* etc. and listening songs of same movies. There were negligible studies at home and pending day by day because of several factors.

The tution problem still remained unsolved My mummy asked to my aunty that they arranged same teacher at my home so he gave reply that I will take 1000 rupees. My parents said OK. then he replied I will come at alternative days then also my parents gave green signal then finally He said "No" to my aunty. I hate this man. As a result of which I dropped the boards exams of 1992. In summer's 1992 daddy put swing upstairs. From that day onwards besides my parents this is my best friend to which I shared every moment of my life. I also sang ghazals and songs.

1992-93: Till 1992 the elder son and his wife look after the school of the chairman but from '92 onwards His Younger son Joined school after completing his M.B.A from A.M.U, so there were some changes in the study pattern. From time to time, he would come into the class and interact with the students. He asked me what you want to do after Xth, I replied that I will do Diploma Engg. From A.M.U in order to quickly Finish my studies. Teachers were teaching from books instead of giving notes. He ordered that teacher to take tuitions in school after school hours instead of their home. My sister and me also took tuitions. When I grasped the studies and concentrated at self-studies. We came in the evening time. My parents had same routine with some little changes as my cousin went to barielly to take training in hotel as he wanted to go to U.A.E. Now only grand ma was with us. I passed my secondary school in 1993. At my farewell I got the BEST STUDENT award. I was busy in my Preboards and Boards. My cousin and his elder brother went to Dubai and Moscow respectively.

I came to know the name of my disease "Cerebral Palsy" when my father prepared my C.M.O certificate from the hospital for my betterment of my future. From hospital I went to my maternal grandma's house, I went inside as one of my maternal uncles wept infront of his mother thinking that I am not listening. He is same uncle who made me walked in my childhood with help of thread.

After giving my Boards I joined Computer course and I thought to go abroad is any type of carrier, one new point came to my mind and this is my weakness till now when any thing stuck to my mind goes out with very difficulty. This problem is also related with my birth problem. So, I started talking about foreign countries. As my uncle lived in U.A.E from 1979. My mother gave me address of her friend who is living in Carmel, California, U. S. A I wrote a letter to her and she gave me reply. My result came in June, I passed my boards with 56 %.

1993-94: My parents had a mind that when I passed my secondary exams, We will admit him in Dayawati Modi Academy so after passing Daddy and I went there. I wanted commerce but there was only science stream. I was confused but the principal convinced me, I thought P.C.B of XII std is difficult. The school was in the outskirts of the city. Then I stayed with my grand mother to gave relief to my parents and studied for class XII which it was given in 1995. In the mean time I read articles of India Today which is a good magazine of India, I took the January 1989 magzine , So I read about Mr. Manu Chabaria which own's a company named JUMBO Electronics , I was very much impressed with him because he owned a electronics shop in Mumbai but from 1st January 1974 he started his company with the help of four Arabian partners and later he took various sick units of India like Dunlop , Shalimar paints etc. He also owned Shaw Wallace company which is situated on Chowrangee lane, Kolata later it was acquired by My Vijay Mallaya, owner of kingfisher, after his death. Now Jumbo Electronics is managed by his wife. so I realized Common man can also achieve this and not only children of Industrialist. After that whenever I got a chance of reading or watching the interview I never missed it. On October 22nd 1993 my cousin joined Unilever in Dubai and he is in same company till date. I also heard ghazals of jagjit singh.

1994-96: One day my father told me his friend brother who was in Pakistan International Airlines (PIA) who was later posted in Dubai as a station in charge of Dubai Airport and Now he is in Florida, U.S.A , I also preserved him in my mind.

I said to my mother I was feeling bored in the house and I want to join Green Wood along with my XII Boards. My

Father talked to chairman and he said you can send him; my father has a good relation with him but I never took an Undue advantage with him. I went to office and I was working, one day my classmate came there and said the authorities gave this register to you for spoiling as my handwriting was bad so after coming home that day, I decided I will not go tomorrow as I am handi. In '94 the school started the eleventh std in P.C.M and P.C.B so my parents put option in front of me why don't you joined P.C.B with Economics instead of doing XII from U.P board so my sister and I

took the admission. So, I lost my two valuable years of my life because of that bloody classmate.

I had not done so well but my small, weak sister managed my studies. she wrote the notes and we both learnt at home. In XII my sister and me got a compartment in physics and Biology But we got good marks in other subjects. So, my father took us to Dehradun for compartment papers. My sister passed in physics but I failed again because I didn't make any diagrams. In both years I enjoyed to study economics. I got good marks in Eco. My sister got good marks in every subject especially in English she also wrote English poems when she was in VI std.

In 1994, another cousin got a chance in Air India, I thought he was sitting at the airport. At that time, I didn't know about city offices as I thought airlines are only confined to airport only but later when I went into depth I knew more about it. I put a stamp on my decision that I will join airlines.

1996-97: In 1996 I got a cycle and I was very happy, Now I thought I am in line of normal children but I was wrong. However, I took a ride of city. I filled the form of I.com from U.P. Board. I was also taking the interest in tution of commerce and I went from my new BSA SLR cycle. That year I also went to few places without work in fond of it. I got a cycle six Yrs.later than my cousins and my classmates. My cycle was a evident of my every tonting etc. till 2010. In 2010 I purchased a new ranger cycle. When every boy purchased scooter, motorbikes I ride on my old cycle seeing them with curiosity. My cycle also felt guilty, the rider will not purchase any bike because of his weakness. I gave my cycle to servant of my neighbourer now my cycle and I say "Hello" to each other whenever I look at my cycle. We both remembered long relationship of 14 years. I passed in my I. Com with IInd division.

1997-2002: In 1997 I took admission in Raza Post Graduate Degree College in commerce faculty, in the same college where my parents took their Bacherlor's and Master's degree. When I went to college for the first time I went to Liabrary where my maternal grandfather spent his entire life, I admired and touched some of the things with a feeling that HE touched all these recks and shelves. My parents told me that he helped students in a very Unique manner. The classes were not conducted in an orderly manner. I went to the professor house for taking tuition. But the exams were conducted in fair and fine atmosphere. I passed my B.com Ist and IIIrd year in 1998 and 2000 respectively in one attempt but I attempted so many times for my B.com IInd year because of my poor handwriting and due to Income tax.

I completed my B.Com in 2002. In all the years it was so difficult to reached the end of answer sheet, when principal took round, He asked me what are you writing and your handwriting is so bad that how will examiner will be able to read it? I told him I am handicapped and if I write in nice way than How I would be able to complete my paper. He said to me then why don't you not join school of handicapped in Jaipur, then I again replied after that school I will have to remain in this society. He said to me sent your father tomorrow. My father went and He praised my thinking and they talked about me. I am regular viewer of "Musafir Hoon Yaroon" which was telecast on star plus on Sunday and anchored by renowed model and actress Deepti Bhatnagar. She traveled to South East Asia like Thailand, Malayasia, Australia, Middle east like U.A.E, and African nations like Egypt, Kenya, South Africa, Seychelles etc. She used Emirates airlines as an official carrier for most of destinations.

Chapter 6:
2002-2012

After giving my B.com IInd year exam ,My mummy's friend nephew called and gave cutting of Sita Academy in which I pursed my airlines course. My parents and I went to Academy before one day, it was May 6th 2002. In Academy Principal asked me about my English and basic knowledge about computers Then I said it is fine. I asked my principal that I will face any type of problem in getting the job and she said Priyanka kakkar who is visually impaired did course from our institute and She got a Job in Stic Travels Pvt. Ltd. I took the admission in International Ticketing and Computerized Reservation System (CRS), Amadeus package which is quite prevalent in India. Amadeus is basically from Spain but in India It is Introduced by Mr. Ankur Bhatia, the owner of Birds Travels. I enjoyed this course and I completed course within span of six months. In between the course I thought that I will Join Birtish Airways or some other airlines like Mahan Air of IRAN etc but not small Travels. I wanted big travels like Stic Travels, Interglobe, Minar Travels. After classes I walked in Connought palace to see different airlines offices and Travel agencies. The things which I heard in Rampur I originally saw offices, it was my little achievement and I thought my fortune has come back which I missed in 1990 but I was wrong. In 2002 in between my course my uncle came to India for a visit, he wanted to reconfirm the ticket. He asked Do you know the office of Syrian Airlines then he and I went to Ambadeep building for recornformation. The boy who confirmed ticket, I assumed that I am doing ticketing, he was also little handy then I was reconfirmed I will definitely get a chance. When our family went to Nirula's to have Sunday's and cold drinks I shared with my mother.

But my fate moved in against direction but in our religion, it is our belief that in every condition we must accept our fate happily in every Ups and Downs.

After course one of my uncles told my father that he should go to Gulf Air and meet Mr. Munnawar Haziq. He took my C.V but he talked with me very negatively. Most of people said You choose the wrong Track and others said You don't have experience? I replied to them If I will choose any other field then I will also face same difficulty. I would reply for the second question regarding experience that I didn't get a proper job till now, So, how can I have experience.

I went to Moradabad for six months in A.B.I Tours and Travels (IATA) But owner of the company did not give proper work according to my profile. He allowed me to sit in his office due to the pressure of some important client and He also gave me one year experience certificate. What is the use of this certificate.

I went to stic travels to submit my C.V.I also want to meet Mr. Subhash Goyal, Chairman but unfortunately his secetary failed for giving the appointment. He met me at once when he came from his office. I personally requested him to give few prercious moments to me but he said Come to me through a proper channel but I failed to meet and convinced him till date.

Stic travels pvt. Ltd. is one of the biggest travel agencies in India. It was started from a small office at Janpath hotel in 1974 to big office at Connought place. It was inaugurated by the former Maharaja of Kashmir Dr. (Mr.) Karan Singh. From 1974 till now it didn't look behind. It own's various Gernal sales Agent (GSA) like Continental airlines, Sri Lankan Airlines, Thai airways, Royal Nepal Airlines, Balkan Bulgarian Airlines etc. and it also represents various Hotels of the world. He wore suits with a hanky in his blazer throughout the year and came to his office from his evergreen car of world i.e Mercedes, in a nutshell He is a very aristocrat man. He is my Ideal. He holds a doctorate for his book "Poverty Eradication and Economic Development through Tourism", the foreword for which was written by Sir Richard Branson, Chairman of Virgin group of Companies, United Kingdom. The then Deputy Prime Minister of India, Mr. L.K. Advani released this book in 2001.

In 2003, there was a job in Air India Charters limited (AICL), a subsidiary of Air India and the interview was held in Centeur hotel but I was rejected because I didn't have DGCA certificate. Then again, I was appeared in written test. In 2010 there was walk in interview in Air India transport services limited (AIATSL) but there was no handicapped quota in it.

In 2006 my father sent me in a travel agency in Delhi. It is a small travel but for me it is one of biggest agency which gave me practical knowledge of my course. It is owned by a nice fellow Mr. S.A. Khan of my city. He made bookings by me, so I was very happy.

He also sent to various airlines offices like Air India, Lufthansa, Syrian Arab airlines, Saudi Arab airlines. I also talked on phone to various offices for the conformation of tickets and they also clearly understood from the other end. I also went to Virgin Atalantic of U.K. through somebody and I talked to Manager for quite a long time, he appreciated my C.V and talking but at the end of talk he told If your voice is up to mark then I wouldn't hesitate to give you job just now but you are facing a difficulty in interacting with the Britishers.

Mr. S.A. Khan of Silk travels also sent me for update of Amadeus package to Birds Travels I wish for him one day He will own a big Travel agency.

Till 2006 I attended three tourism conferences. Out of them two held in Ashoka hotel and one in Intercontinental in Connought Palace.

In 2006, My cousin Mrs. Reena daughter of Mrs Raj kumari Indira Mohini sent me to one of her friends who is advocate and run's a big law company then she sent me to Mrs. Radha Bhatia wife of Ankur Bhatia, I met her but as usual she gave negative reply. Birds Travels is own's a GSA of Lufthansa German Airlines.

I was out of touch from travel trade from 2006.

In 2009, I took off on 2nd Janaury at 19:00 hrs from the flight of Air Arabia with my friend cousin with an excitement and having the pleasure of drinking cola in a beautiful glass. We had a long chat till the landing of aircraft on Sharjah International airport. On 3rd my cousin and I went on terminal 3 which is exclusively for Emirates Airlines to received my cousin family. From 3rd, in car I calculated when I will go back to India and I missed my parents. On 4th Jan I joined my office as an Accountant and on same day I went to Al- Ain to meet my uncle. With passing of days, I was involved in my work with daily telephonic conversation from my parents. I also saw the various malls and other Places of Dubai. I understood all my work profile but I took help of my Immediate boss like holes in paper, staples of paper etc. due to the shaking of my hands. My boss didn't like this although my uncle talked about me. So, when one Indian boy also joined my company in March, in April My boss told me in a good atmosphere Why don't you start your business in India. As you already have exposure of outside world. With all these matters along with some other personal matters which is not solved by me I came back to India. I took the flight on 12th July 2009 from Dubai International Airport –Terminal 1 of Air India. I went to airport much before the flight to adhere the decoration of airport. I was accompanied by my bhabhi's cousin. I again enjoyed perhaps the last flight of my life. I requested airhostess to look into the cockpit of aircraft. When I saw my parents after eight months, my mummy sinked after looking, she was O.K. at that time but she was hospitalized after coming to Rampur. Every relative told me she missed you very much. My Father also missed but he is so courageous man that no body can guess what he is feeling but my sister and me entirely upon my mother.

After coming from Dubai my parents decided for me to tie a Knot and on March 4th March 2010, I married at Taj Palace, Rampur. For the first time I wore Sherwani in which I looked smart and on 6th of march I wore suit and red tie.

Tie is still my weakness, In B.com I thought I will wear a tie and tie a Knot daily at my airlines office but it is still a dream.

In 2012 I called for my job to my uncle and after few days he called for a job in Indian Islamic Cultural (IICC) in delhi in Accounts department and Director who joined this center after retirement from Centur Hotel was also interested in my job. My accounting manager did not take keen interest in me. I worked there for about 15 days. This is from my background that when somebody hits my self-respect, I can't tolerate it.

This is not a world of handicapped but nobody can't take their life because it is a gift of GOD but there is no acceptance in society. From my childhood till I am spending my married life I was nowhere. I am just in mid of ocean, searching the bank of ocean but when I swim that much the bank looks very far from my approach. Now I have no further plans in my mind How I will spend my entire life. Handicapped should study only for awareness, Vision billa billa but don't set any target after looking at normal ones. Now I am like a stagnant water and no one to put pebbles in it.

The building of my career was started fallen which our parents and I made sensibly, carefully and with other precautionary measures but we thought we managed it but we were wrong. We put later bricks on the hallow place. Hallow space can't be filled. As a result of this I dropped it for the first time in 1992 and from that time I was waiting for that train......... sometimes I meet passengers of the train, I wanted to board throughout my life, but on rushing train never slowed down for me. I am like the stranded traveler waiting on the platform of this world for my chance to come and I laid down on memory lanes.

My Ideals

My ideals and Their Works : The ideal personas are those to whom you want to make your life like them but its your luck you achieved that target or not . When I was in school and college, after completing my Xth std. in'93 I was Impressed many people like to go foreign countries as my two cousins went to U.A.E and Russia but One of my father's friend's sons joined Air India. Upto 12th I was confused then I was confirmed to go in the airlines industry.

Mrs. Akhtar Jahan: This is universal truth that Mother lap is first school of every child. My Mother is of sacrificing nature. When she married her father gave some tips how you spend your life and she obeyed. She received respect in return in every relation whether in her house and in laws but not as much according to me. She perfectly managed her college and house life. She deserved more.

Her professional carrier was up to the mark, she gave her valuable and precious 37 years to college named as N.M.G.I.C. After completing her education (B.A) from Post graduate Raza Degree college, After B.A she joined N.M.G.I.C Then She went to Aligarh to pursed B.ED. When she came back, she wants to joined other colleges but her father refused. So, she joined the same college. From "62 to 84 she was in L.T. grade, many clerks asked my grand pa If You say Yes Then I will try for her lecturer grade then both of them refused. In "84 she got Lec.grade and she became

History Lectuter (1984-99). As I am handicapped, my father and She brought up me in a normal atmosphere. They sent me in Regular school and college. They didn't prejudice between my sister and me.

Till now when her students met in parties, they gave warm welcome and said You are my ideal.

My collegue asked me from where you get sacfrificing nature I proudly said from my mother i.e. Akhtar Jahan Begum.

Her stories are published in many magazines and in last she wrote a book "APNA HI GHARMA BHOOL GAYE". One professor of Raza Degree college published Rampur ke Afsanagar, He also took one of story of Akhtar Jahan Begum

Mr. (DR.) M.G. Rayee: I knew him from 2004 when his sister and Brother-in-law came to our house and proposed my sister. All things were going in a positive way and tie a knot on 8th October, 2004.

He is Cardithrocic surgeon and he is Head of Depament in Patna Medical college and Hospital (P.M.C.H)

He told my sister that when You came in my life, I got a fellowship from Australia. But due to some obstacles he went there in 2006. When he came back on 26th may 2006 his son (Wasif) open eyes in this world. Before 2006 he and my sister went to Mauritius He also attending many conferences throughout the year in India and abroad. He went with entire family. His present and future both are good.

He is very Kind hearted man. Like my parents and sister, from timc to time he called me and boost my morale.

When ever we all consult Docters, he didn't interrupt the docter as he shown that I am also docter.

Mr. Farhat Ullah Khan: When one boy opens his eyes on 1.9.44 in Mr. and Mrs.Qudrat Ullah Khan's lap nobody knows what he achieved in his life.

As life moves, he took admission in Post Graduate Raza Degree college in B.A. At that time Agra and Rohilkhand university was one, so there were many colleges. In 1961 He topped Agra University. Then he went Aligarh Muslim University (A.M.U) for pursing M.A(English). The Vice Chance. Gave warm welcome by shaking hand. He completed his M.A and Joined A.M.U as a Lecturer from 1963 -65.

He again came and joined Aligarh Muslim University. When Aligarh opened campus in U.A.E, He went there for short Span and he came back. He also Head of Dept. (H.O.D) in English Dept. He also nominated for post of V.C but in the last he didn't select. Along He was a good professor, he also suits for administrative job according to his personality. After retirement he went to K.S.A as a principal in Delhi Public school. He was a local Gurdian of my sister when she pursed M.A (English). Now the colleges and universities sent invitation for his lectures. The Aligarh standard style is having beautiful Residence and an Italian Fiat car. His residence name is "Gul Numa". In '18 Raza Degree College gathered those persons who achieved extraordinary carrier and He is one of them. His Dressing sense is subereb whether in western dress or in Rampuri dreesing. He is very helpful to all persons especially to persons from Rampur.

After his death he got award RAMPUR RATAN which his daughter received on his behalf.

Mr. Azhar Inayti: Rampur is considered as a Urdu school after Delhi and Lucknow. Many peots (shayar) put a name of Rampur on the International platform.

Mr. Azhar Inayati completed his L.L.B From A.M.U when he came back, he didn't practice Law. He chooses Shayari (poetry). His mentor was Mr. Inyati. I met with him in '90 for first time. I like him. He gave his book to my father. He told to my father that I am going to U.S. He also visited like Dubai, Oman, many places of U. S, Canada etc. He also attended that Mushaira, we also saw this Mehfil on V.C.R that held in Dubai (U.A.E) in honour of Mr. Joan Aliya, from Amoroha. Mr. Mauj Rampuri also attened that Evening.

Mr. Azhar is owner of beautiful poetry like

RAASTON KIYA HUYA WHO LOG, JO AATE JAATE MERE ADAB PE KEHTA THE KE JETE RAHYA.

JABSE BATAYA HAI NUJUME NE MERE NAAM, APNI HATIYOLI KO DEKITA NAHIN KOI.

Now, he shows keen intrest in Natiya Shiyari. In 2020, The Mushaira held in honour of Mr. Azhar Inayati under banner of *JASHN–E- INYATI* in Doha, Qatar. He received a shawl and cheque of Rs. One lakh. In this context I must say this is honour of Rampur.

Mrs. Junita Zaki: LA Montessri school Started by S.N Bhatia. At that time, He opened branches to various Places. Rampur Branch took by Raza Textile Pvt.Ltd and It was managed by the wife of Mr. V.K Srivastava (Joint M.D).

My Father was Public Relation Officer and he also saw Human Resources Activities (H.R) in Raza textiles.

Mr Zaki joined the Company. He was in Marketing and Sales Dept. in Raza Textiles Pvt. Ltd. After some time, Mrs. Junita Zaki joined school and soon she became principal. Later when the tie up with LA Montessri was finished, and name was changed to stepping stones.

Mrs. Zaki managed the school in such a beautiful and smoothing way. In Meerut she took degree Classes. She participated in all activities whether it is Annual function, she also introduced to speak thought of day in front of school in assembly, putting important news on board. She also managed to go company's club to saw cartoon and Movies. Sometimes she sent to Raza Textiles and on 14th Nov. she arranged picnic for us. She and Entire staff didn't hit my sentiments whether it was cricket or Annual function. She is a dignified and soft-spoken lady.

When both the sons of Mr. V.K went to Doon Schoo l, Mrs. VK's introduced Same syllbus in our School. Mrs Zaki also took some English classes. Mrs.Vk's forsightness helped us.

When the company shut its operation.

In '94 Mr.and Mrs.Zaki started their school St. Anotony. In the first year they recognized the Xth boards. With in short span, they introduced 11th class in science (P.C.B & P.C.M) and Commerce stream They also opened junior branch.

Whenever I went there, they supported me. For Amway they arrange meeting of entire Staff in both branches. And secondly when I was in New York Insurance, I went with my collegue she shown intrest.

Now my uncle (Mr. Zaki) is not in this world. Yet her journey is not over, she also opened third Branch.

People took long time to established their business, what she did in short span.

Azeem Akbar: He is my ideal. When he was in St. Mary's He usually came to my house mostly on Sunday.

My parents welcome him, as my father respect his father. When My sister and I came to upper classes he also saw my books and guide us from time to time.He completed His 10th std from St.Mary's ,Then he moved to Raza Inter College ,He choose commerce streme .Then he joined Raza Degree Post Graduate college to pursued B.Com .After completing he went Aligarh Muslim University (AMU) for Master of Business Administration (M.B.A).

When he completed M.B. A programme he Joined Hamdard in Delhi in '92. He married in Feb. 1993. Within span of one year, oppourtunity came and he joined Air India in '94.

From '94 to till date he is in same company. He is holding post Asst.gernal manager (personnel). When I went to gave interview of Air India Charters Limited (AICL) he sat there for taking interview in Centur Hotel. He is having good personality. I also went to his house he and his family welcome me. He is very genrous and kind, there was a paper of AICL in Salwan public school one handicapped person asked him some question, so he sat near him and told him.

He is very down to earth. He is devotee and dedicated to work.

Mr. Sheeraz Hasan khan: He is my cousin. His father was working in HAL in Kanpur (U.P). He is one brother and sister. His schooling was very nice. So, he is soft spoken with a good English. He is also helping nature.

He completed his 10th and 12th grade in '89 and '91 resp. As in consecutive year he completed his B.SC in 1994. As soon as he completes his graduation he got job in Novraties, a Multinational Pharma company. It is one of ten best company in world. He is in Marketing Dept. He served for about 7 to 8 years in this company. During job he also joined M.B.A programe from Symbosis collge in Lucknow campus. He transferred to Lucknow, Jhansi etc.

After serving Pharma company He went to U.A.E. There he was in Mineral water company but he didn't statisfy. Then he came back to India and joined Call Center. Again, the opportunity came in his way, He went to Saudia Arabia (K.S.A). Firstly, he joined Luna Juices and finally he joined Glass company. He is stationed in Riyadh, but he is having touring job in different countries like Central America, Middle east, African & European Countries etc.

Mr. Mohd. ALI KHAN: He studied in Greenwood Senior Sec. School from L.KG to 10th std. The school was recognized only when his bacth was in xth std. In 1990 he completed 10th std. then he moved to Moradabad to pursed commerce from English medium, but he came back and joined Raza Inter college. In 1992 he successful completed his 12th grade. In 1992 he joined B. Com in Raza Degree P.G

College. In 1995 he completed his Bachelor course. He came to my house while talking he said without wasting any year in my life I completed my B.Com.

He searched job but when he waited train to came to Rampur, In the meantime he saw vacancy in Hyatt regency, He went there and fortunately he got job. This Hotel is U.S based and It is located through out the world. I saw buildings of this hotel in Delhi and Dubai, both are beautifully designed.

After he served Hyatt for 7 years, then he went to Dubai. He worked in many hotels in Mumbai, Bangalore and various countries of Middle east. After Hyatt, he worked in Taj, Intercontinental (Now the Lalit), Radisson SAS etc. Every time, he got better position and designation then previous. When he met last and he gave me his card, he was Director of Marketing.

He is very artistic type of person and sentimental. I enjoyed when I talked to him. He fond of listening Ghazals and good movies. He want to go different places and talk to different peoples. He is soft spoken. He is also helpful nature.

Mr. Khan: He is my child hood friend till date. but our classmate journey was finished in 6th std. I went to Green Wood sr.sec school from where my failures were started and I say good bye to my luck in Stepping Stone school.

His good luck is still with him. After 8th std. from the same school, he went to Minto Circle (A.M.U) and completed his 12th grade from there. His writing is upto mark in 6th std. and grasping power is also good.

In 1994 he joined engg. And complted on the scheduled time. Then After engg. He joined Oswal Fertilisers in Shahjanpur, U.P then he moved to Dubai (U.A.E) for some time. He came back along with his determination he went to Saudia Arabia (K.S.A) and joined SABIC company. But Now He joined Philips chervolt.

From 1988 till today we met only 4 times but whenever we meet, we linkup talks from there only where we finished. He also having good personality.

Junaid Hadi, His younger brother is in Alana group, Bombay based company. He is M.B.A., He is good Profile and designation.

I wish all the best of luck for above personalities for their future. I just appreciated their efforts because GOD helps only those who help themselves. Work satisfaction, efforts and dedication are the most important elements, if it is not then person worked for whole life but there is no charm.

Navaid………..

My First Voyage Experience

When I was On departure Terminal at Delhi airport ,I Looked at my parents expressions, who were giving final tips with their loneliness in their hearts that when again they will meet me? Clock was going faster and faster. Finally, my check in time came, I entered the airport waving hands to them. I disappeared in the strange crowd that were to accompany me for a little time with whitish colour of my parents' hairs. I arrived for the first time at the SHARJAH International Airport, SHARJAH on Jan. 2nd 09 by Air Arabia. For the first time I stepped from the aircraft admiring Arab architecture and their cleanliness and their maintenance in each and every corner that amazed me. I first walked on wooden flor to collect my Visa on the counter then I moved further for other formalities of the Airport. In the queue I admired the official Cabins with paperless tables, L.C.D screens and Comfortable Chairs while talking to my cousin who had come with me from India. The big hall was designed with arch dome architecture. On 3rd Jan, my cousin and I Went to Terminal 3 at Dubai International airport to receive my cousin's family, Terminal 3 is specifically built for the Emirates Airlines. In the mean time we went to DEIRA City center. From 4th Jan I joined my office. After office hours I would usually go to see different places by buses and sometime with my cousin and also with my colleagues. I visited different malls like Dubai mall, mall of

Emirates etc. I saw Terminal 2, which is for low-cost Carrier, and to near by Destination from Dubai. I spent there two hours, it is first airport of Dubai and is being renovated. The airlines offices and other offices are built as well as renovated in such a nice way. Airlines offices built up of Red colour. I went to cafeteria, took one Pepsi from fridge and thinking about past when my uncle came here for the first time at UAE on Terminal1 30 years back. Dubai as well as UAE has Changed tremendously. I sat on the comfortable seats of the Departure Terminal feeling people are going to their homes and I missed my family Very much.

I was living in Dubai and usually in the weekend I used to go to my cousin in Sharjah. On returning from SHARJAH my cousin's wife took new driving license. We went for a long drive to UMM Al QWAIN Via AJMAN and they all give me introduction and wanted me to be familiar with roads and places which are on our way and in late night they dropped me at my room in Dubai and from Saturday I resumed my services again. I liked my cousin's locality ABU SHAGARA. In the weekend I usually sat on Abu Shagara Park Which is very well maintained and there is Staff to look after the park. The grass is neatly trimmed with trees of KHAJJOR (date palms trees) on lanes of park and lamppost with white lights. It seems that Entire India is codenzed into one park, Children playing on the swings and birthdays are organized in that park.

When I Visited Dubai mall, I went to back side of the mall from where I saw Burj Dubai which is not officially opened. The Burj holds the record of tallest building in world and it is Visible from every corner of Dubai. The height of Burj Dubai is 818 m (2684 ft.). I used to watch Bruj Dubai from my office balcony.

According to me, Dubai is city of malls; they built malls on international standards with every facility. The latest innovation they developed was PALM ISLAND in the Ocean, it was not an easy task but they managed it some how because I saw construction Documentary on Discovery Channel. They appointed European and American Engg. They are not limited to only residential colonies on island but they construct ATLANTIS Hotel in that island. I visited with my uncle and his Wife, who came from U. S. Atlantis is spread into big Area in front of ocean and it is summary of big castle or Fort. I also saw the pictures; ATLANTIS is inaugurated in between most expensive fireworks of the world. The Entrance Fee is 300AED Per Person. The BURJ Al ARAB is the first seven-star hotels in Dubai as well as in UAE. The Dubai Govt. Built Departure and Arrival Terminal only for National Carrier "Emirates" in addition to terminal1 and 2, which is only Terminal in Asia and Uncommon in Europe and America (as Per my knowledge is Concerned) but unfortunately, I didn't see this terminal from inside. The new airport of Dubai in Jebel Ali is under construction which is going to open soon. I like view of Buildings of Sheikh Zayed road from the car it seems that every building is reply of another building and we are passing through some fairy land especially at night. My Colleague, Mr. Nisar Ahmed told me there is only World Trade Center building on this road and tallest Building in Dubai but Now that White Building is bending, telling their age and bless young sky creppers and maintain their dignity by saying this "I am history of this road as well as Dubai." I went to deira as well as Bur dubai Creek. There I got impression of old Dubai Because it was an important Trading Point in early 60's. People used to move by boats between Deira and Bur dubai and this practice is common till date When Bur and Deria Dubai are Connected by Road through SHANDIGA Tunnel.In the evening time people used to came and relax their mind because moving water gives relax of mind with waves coming on shore. People used to sit in Cafeterias and watched Fireworks, During this time all people close together and stop every activity and shoot fireworks from their mobile and camcoders. There are also dining Ships which are decorated beautifully with a light music. Both Sides are having tall buildings which looked more beautiful from opposite sides especially Rolex Building. The local name of creek is "ABRA". By seeing Traditional boats, I remembered the old days what I heard from elders when traders sat along the shore and wait for their Products. In some boats lateerns are hanging. By seeing lateerns on boats I used to hum the song "O mahjee RE Tera Sahara koi ...." I used to drink pepsi or tea on railing and watching people going on boats to BUR DUBAI or coming to DEIRA. I liked the names of roads which are kept on names of capital cities of gulf countries like Damascus Road, which was my office street, Doha Road, Beirut street etc., and I liked names of different roundabouts like fish and cockroach round abouts on which artifical fishes are desingned & decorated with lights and Big & Small Cocraches with their eggs respectively.

I came to India by Air India Flight 746 from Dubai International Airport, Terminal 1 on 12th July ,09. My Cousin dropped me at the airport at 19:30. Then I went inside the airport. My cousins, Bhabhi, my nephew Adnan and I came from the same car at 19:00 but after half an hour they and I moved in opposite direction. We all disappeared from one another. I screened my luggage, then moved to air India counter to check in my luggage. My bhahbi's brother came with me on same flight. After taking our boarding pass, we moved towards Dubai Duty Free Shop through escalators, some of the passengers moved through Cable cars. Then finally through stairs I saw the huge shop with variety of one product which were displayed in a beautiful in such a manner that a person will buy an article compulsorily. From my childhood I felt fumes of ROTHMANS and DUNHILL so

I moved to the cigrate shelve and saw different brands of cigarette.

I admired they decoration which was done in beautiful manner and on international standards. People were busy in shopping but I was busy in watching every corner. The entire airport seemed as if was bathing in lights and Mashals were engraved into walls with beautiful Flame. I saw a hand bag for Mummy but I was not able to purchase it as it was quite expensive. Then I went to 2nd floor towards the gate 106, passengers were waiting on comfortable sofas for their flights, kids were on their prams, we walked on the wooden floor, clicking videos from mobile of artificial national Trees with dim lights. Finally, we said GOOD BYE to the Dubai Airport and by showing my boarding pass my co partner and I moved inside aircraft where I smelled the Fragnance of INDIA after six months. My seat No. was 10 E and my Bhabi's brother also seated near me by giving his seat to another passenger who was seated near me. On the Window seat the principle of Gems school was going to Kolkata via Delhi. We talked to them then air hostess announced to fasten seat belts, Captain names and aircraft took off from Dubai airport. We swithched on the ghazals and on the small screen in front my seat I saw the aircraft movement till Delhi airport, it also showed altitude we are flying, outside temperature, Hours Remaining to reach destination and Current location on which aircraft is flying. When we moved our head aircraft service Started, one smart Steward served drinks to passenger from front to middle and two air hostess served drinks from back to middle and same operation went going on in First Class in a cheerful mood in an Indian Style and Indian hospitality which is famous all over World. We all three took cold drinks with ice cubes. I looked at Air hostees and Steward in a very Curisioty because I wanted to serve Airlines. I asked Few questions to steward without taking his precious time and he answered very gently and politly. After drinks dinner was served with a cup of coffee. After dinner passenger were taking long nap, some is reading magazines I went to wash room with little chat with official of when he joined the organization billa billa. Finally, we landed on the Delhi airport. Then after landing we took some time inside airport that my Parents also Knew that, who were sitting in Visitor lounge but their eyes searching for their son in every passenger finally we entered the lounge area with bhabhi's brother and I saw my parents after six months and I Joined my parents whom I missed in Dubai. Our car moved to my city while I chatted with my parents. I wish India will have seprate departure and arrival terminal for National carrier **Air India** in the near future .

Memory Lanes

I went to my maternal uncle house, he purchased a car recently so I convinced him for a long drive. We are confused Where we Go! In end We finialised For the Exhibition which is in local language it is called "NUMAISH" it was started during the Nawab's time Because Rampur is small city but it was Nawab state. It was also called SANAATI and ZRAATI exhibition.

I went to exhibition from my Childhood with my elder maternal Uncle who was in All INDIA RADIO (AIR), and He was on duty but he arranged in a systematically

way that he took family members especially my aunt and me, who left a brutal world on 3rd Nov. 2013. I sat on stage with my maternal uncle and I met with the artist like Manna Day, who expired in 2013 and Tun tun. we also attended Mushaira and Music Conference along with a round in exhibition. My father was in Raza Textiles pvt. ltd, which was having so many units. Artist used to stay in Company Guest House . I was so small my aunt told me that Mr. Talat Aziz came in owner Mercedes car; His Persona is so Great. Mr. Jagjit Singh who was a king of Ghazal Singer introduced him. Mr. Talat Aziz gave so many hits, song like *"ZINDAGI TERI BAZM MEIN LATI HAIN HUMEIN"* and *"Ainna Mujhse pehli si surat Mange"* in Movie Umrao Jan and Daddy (1991) respectively. I also heard Mr. Guru das Mann, who is king of Punjabi Industry. Beside yesterday I went last in

1988, along with my younger maternal uncle, He is very fond of music. On that day Mr. Udit Narayan who just Initated his career, Previously He was Radio announcer in Nepal.He announced I will sing a track from forthcoming film Qamat Se Qamat tak (QSQT) and In this movie new face came in film industry i.e. Mr. Amir Khan and Miss Juhi Chawala from day both of them never looked behind. In 1988 this movie released and hit the screens. From this movie and Maine Pyar Kiya (1989) the trend of movies changed. In same Year my uncle came from AL-AIN with a V.C.R with this movie. He also purchased T.V and entire family watched this movie.

Yesterday when we finalized for a visit to exhibition, so my Maternal uncle arranged a Trip with all my cousin and We picked them. Finally, we land to the Desired Destination. When we enter the gate, which is built like the gate of Aligarh. We heard my favorite track DARD-E –DIL from the movie Karz, which was sung by Golden voice Singer Mr. Mohd. Rafi Sb. We took a round and then We purchased. We all enjoyed according with the ages. Three of the ate Chow Ming, One cousin and I ate Ice Cream (softy) in the local food court. On every step I laid down on memory lanes and we enjoyed songs of early and late eighties. When we left, we heard song "yeah Galiyan ye chaubara" from movie Prem Rog. There was a same popcorn fragrance as we felt in my childhood and my maternal uncle purchased them. My Cousin sat on Camel who is ship of desert.

We went to one bag shop, on that shop one pious girl with entire burkah, I don't know what is reason why she sat on shop. We visited to different shops but display of furniture was very nice so that person should buy definitely like the big shopping malls.

In last We saw motor cycle and cars running in *'Maut ka kuan'* (Death Well). We salute boys who run them and did Gymnastic on moter cycle and cars. I thought these boys who did like this did not get proper renumeration. In Satwaan Asman Which relased in 1992, Vivek Mushroon run motor cycle and in last he died but his soul gave red Duppata to Pooja Butt.This movie was directed by Mr. Shekhar Kapur. The rain was started the we all moved to respected houses. This exhibition should be modified to National or Internaltional standard So that people from near by cities and foreigners also came because they came to our nearby city Moradabad, a Brass city. Now, also airport will start in Moda Panday.The rain was started so we all enjoyed the rain in car on national highway.

Ideal Teachers

Ideal Teachers are those to whom and copy about them. In my life there are only one male teacher and five female teachers. They taught me in this way I liked their way of teaching.

Firstly, our cousin and we (my sister & I) were studied in La Montes (Later Stepping Stones) and then we (our sister &I), studied in Green Wood senior Sec. School from '88 till '96. Our cousins studied one year in G.W.S.S.S & then moved to bly.1989. My one cusion came from Bly. My sister studied one year then she took admission in St. Mary's, my sister completed her Xth std. in '94 from St. Mary's then again, she took admission in Greenwood from '94-'96. I studied from '88- '96. My elder counsin Completed his xth std. in '90 from G.W.S.S.C then moved raza Inter college.

Mr. Irfan Lateef Khan Sb.: belong to respectable family of Rampur. His Father was also a great teacher of his times. His legacy transfer to all his sons. His one son was Asst. Register in Jamia Milia Islamia, Delhi. His one son is a lecturer in Murtaza College, After His retirement he also started his school.

Mr. Irfan Lateef sb.is my Mentor and Philosopher joined stepping school, He taught in class quite good so there was no need of tution. But we took a tuition. When we left school, soon he left school. He also played cricket in free period with my class. When I was in 7th std. He arranged a teacher for us. He prepared us much before the Exam. Along with studies he also gave moral teachings. & he put an eye on all our activities.

When we passed in our final exams, he gave gifts to us and our cousin.

In '94 or in '95 he started own school with a name "LITTLE BUDS" Now also he guided me from time to time.

He also having a good dressing sense and nice hair style.

All brothers stretched his father legacy.

MRS RASHMI: Her father was in Raza Textile. After completing her Bachlor's (B.A), She joined company school. She taught English in a very orderly manner. Before starting a new chapter, she said in class, just learnt difficult spells. Next day she dictated all spellings and check copies immediately so everybody has a rush, how much you got a number. In competation everybody did best.

MY father visits often to her house with Mr. Dabral sb. so she told our performance. Today he got good marks or less marks.

All teachers and Principal never neglected me in anything whether it was cricket, social activities or thought of day. On annual function also we participated.

Mrs. & MR. V.K arranged a birthday party for his sons so all Officer wives, Daughters and officers were there. And enjoyed in their own way according to their own way & according to own ages. My Mother talked to Miss Rashmi,

Miss Farhat Sahiba, Miss Alka. We played musical chairs and other games etc. We ate pakhois and took cold drinks.

On Diwali we also gathered, all kids and gents played fire works & All ladies sat in portoco, with a white table putting a glass of cold drink. But my Mummy prefered Tea. Then we ate dinner and came to our house.

Miss Rashmi: She was my G.K teacher in green wood. She herself found new topics and dictated notes and after one day she asked from entire class one by one. Sometimes she dictates us capital of countries, currencies, longest, highest things etc. She regularly checked copies.

Miss Vinita Singh: Joined Stepping Stones in'87. She was also my English Teacher. All teachers special Care for me but no one point on me now, I realized. She gave us same atmosphere as miss Rashmi. As In winter vacation I went to Ajmer, Jaipur and Agra on my mother's college tour. When school reopen my English teacher asked to write about your vacation. I wrote essay and that was fine. I saw RAJ MANDIR which is a beautiful in Asia.

Mrs Vinita: It was beginning of my Viii std. In first term I got good numbers in all subjects except social science (history, civics & geog.) In July she joined our school. Her teaching method is quite different. She wrote little notes on black board and we, all students note it and prepared entire answers from the residence. She checked it. In this way I got good marks (above 60%) in social science along with other subjects in half yearly exam.

Mrs. Anugrayh: She was my economics teacher, she was a substitute but later she confirmed. She explained in just a beautiful way so every student grasp it whether it was demanding supply, monopoly in market, Statistics etc. I got good marks in economics because I thought that I will do B.com or B.B.A after 12th.

Mrs. Preeti Anand: In '02 when my cousin gave a cutting of starting new course of international tktg. And Computerised reservation system (CRS), Amadeus. My parents and I rushed to institute & I took admission. This duration of this course is about 6 Months. I completed course on time.

From that time, I went from time to time, she does not discourage me but as a contrary she encouraged my confidence level. She also wants to start business but that opportunity didn't mature.

I went to academy on alternate days, so in gap I went to Ansal Plaza, sometimes movies. At that time Devdas, Sur, Humraz was relased.

She is also a humble and kind hearted lady. After sometime she started her own academy. She is having a good knowledge of her subject. In between classes she asked different question of realted topics. As far as I belong to a small town, but also, I gave answers.

From Letters To Email

In past Pigeons was only medium to send message from one place to another . They were trained to go to definite place and returned with Reply. In this way they maintain the links between two person, kings and governors. The kingdom was running very smoothly. The pigeon song *"Kabtoor Ja Ja"* was picturized in movie *"Maine Pyar kiya"* in 1989.

Later when world is progress then Post came into existence, then communication of pigeon is slow down and in due course of time it eliminates from society. After some time, telegram was introduced in connection to give emergency news and in short. Letter took time to deliver for about a month. Letter proves complete source of sentiments in comparison modern technology.

In past all youngster wanted to live in the same city with their parents but when the awareness came and young generation went outside for their further studies and job, within India or Outside.

When my paternal grandfather went to 2nd World War, My grandma wrote letters and showed concern about him and Vice Versa.

In '61 When my mother went to A.M.U My maternal grandmother wrote reguralry and when my mother sent reply, she posted letter next day. When my mother wants to study more, she didn't allow her.

My two maternal and one paternal uncle, went to Aligarh for studies. Then my one maternal went to Jammu & Kashmir in ALL INDIA RADIO and second maternal uncle went to Kolkata. My paternal uncle went to Al-Ain, U.A.E. Then my both grandmothers sent letters regularly. After sometime my one elder maternal uncle came to Rampur and other uncle changed his job and he was nearby stations, so he came on every weekend. My paternal uncle spent 33 years in U.A.E, So, my granny wept and letter practice was going on regularly.

There are different types of envelops for within India and outside India. My paternal grandmother wrote letter on big envelop like Air mail etc. With in India there are Post card and Inland letters.

My parents asked me to write letter to all of them, so your English will up to the mark.

Post & Telegram Dept. is a government organization and Postman is important element. He Knows every language and wearing brown uniform with a typical bag. He went door to door for delivering letters. Before 50 years our society is illetrate so he read letters and also wrote. In recent past when new innovation is coming in market, this dept. also upgraded. Uptil today many things are attached to Post office like draft, Government entrance forms, etc. The letter song was also picturized in movie Shakti, Deedar-e-Yaar etc.

Courier companies have come into market and they are prevailing in market like DHL, First Flight, Desk to Desk, Overnite, Gati etc. Big Courier companies are having their own aircrafts. They also deliver letters, important document on time.

In 1998 the latest innovation was Email. It is fastest medium to communicate with parents, friends and relatives. There are many companies in market to create an Email account as well as you know email address of that particular person and the companies are Yahoo, rediff, Hotmail. It takes small time for receiving the reply. Then chatting on yahoo messenger came in way, People also enjoyed it.

Email and chatting were introduced in movie Dil hi dil mein, which was released in 1998. I created my email account in 2000 on Yahoo and now my account on gmail. Through Web cam we also saw our dear ones.

In 2004 the Face Book was introduced and I joined it in 2010. In this you will create the account and you will give small information about yourself. In this you are online 24 hours. You put comment, likes and if any secrecy then use inbox. In Email it took a time for about 4 to 5 hours but on facebook, reply took no time, but condition is person is online.

For introduction of any new innovation in the society, Movies are best platform because masses are concern about it.

8'o clock

It was morning of 30th of march when we planned a trip to Patna where my sister got married to Dr.MD.Gheyas rayee on 8th Oct.2004. My parents one maternal Uncle and I came here on their reception in Chankaya Hotel. I went with my Parents in 2008 but for two days. In 2014 We went there for quite a long time almost a month. We took a Shermjeevi rail from our nearby city Moradabad at 16:30. The origin and destination point are Delhi and Calcutta resp. As we waited for a train, I took a cold drink to pass a time. A train came and we started our journey accompanied with two jawans of Border Security Force (BSF) with a destination point at Bareilly, with a no stoppage at Rampur, **I have forwaded a request with Ministry of Railways (MOR) and officials of railways Please consider my humble request in connection with a stoppage at Rampur so the passenger will not catch the train from Bareilly or Moradabad.** The rail will reach at Luckow at 22:00 from there one I.A.S accompanied us. He and my father talked over a cup of tea. We arrived at Danapur around10:00'O clock, a one stop before Patna junction because Patna Junction crowded place. Our brother-in-law at the station so we headed towards the house. My sister waited for us eagerly. we had breakfast then we looked their renovated house. On Saturday the elder members of family went to Gopalganj, a nearby hilly area to attend a marriage of of my sister's sister-in-law with 6 hours' drive from Patna. In evening the children of my sister, sister –in –law along with me went to YO! China. There we ate Chinese cuisine along with coke. One day my sister and I went to Nine 2 Nine to purchase some essential commodities. On next Sunday My brother–in–law, maternal nephew and I went to school to give her medical prelims. Then we took her and came to house with a little stay at Rayee Nursing Home. I admired his chamber. He is having two nursing homes. I went with him to Patna Medical college and hostpital (PMCH), In both places his subordinates gave me warm welcome. I was pleased to see his designation as Associate Prof.along with M.S. On Sunday evening the entire family went to KFC.It Way back in 1930 colonel Harland sanders got some dilicious. Kentucky folk licking their fingers. We all enjoyed very much along with strange crowd. We saw two movies Mein Tera Hero and 2 States in Cinnepolis.The auditorium are well maintained and I saw for the first time, the steward asked for the order. The cinnepolies is located in P&M mall. The mall is beautifully designed. Cinepolis is 4th largest chain of PVR in the world. We went to Madras café to have a bite of dosa. I enjoyed Pepsi IPLT20 with a tag line" Chalo Bhulava aaya hai". which was held in different cities of U.A.E like Abu Dhabi, capital of Emirates, Dubai and Sharjah, Now It continue in different cities of India and hot election discussion on NDTV 24*7 and Times Now.I decided to take a domestic flight and came before my parents from Jaiprakash Narayan international airport. I purchased stand by ticket from Indigo. Indigo is Gurgoan based airlines started by Rakesh Gangwal and Rahul Bhatia. The parent company is Interglobe Enterprises. Its IATA code is 6E and Hello 6E is its inflight magazine. It was founded in 2006 and commenced its operation from 4th August 2006. Its primary hubs are Indira Gandhi International airport. Secondary hubs are Chattrapati Shivaji International Airport, Mumbai and Netaji Subhash Chandra Bose International Airport, Kolkata. The focus cities are Lucknow, Cheenai, Banglore etc. The fleet size is 78.The airline offers 491 daily flights with 36 destination.It alsoflew to Bangkok, Dubai, Singapore, Oman, Kathmandu. Then I waited in lounge ,at18:oo hrs for security then the ground staff handed over my boarding pass and I moved ahead towards boarding hall then after waiting for half an hour I moved towards aircraft through Indigo bus .It was a awesome experience for me to take a first domestic flight. MY seat is 21E. Then plane take off from grassy field in the sky at 8'o clock. There was a bidding system and selling of eatable items like sandwiches, burgers and coke. Then the regular sevices of air hostess started till landing on Delhi airport. When I saw ariel view of Delhi from plane, It was amazing. After landing I collected luggage from Belt No.5. That was how my 8 O'clock came to good ending and smooth landing.

Advertising

Advertising is a medium through which company inform the public with existing product and new launch . Company spends a hefty amount in advertising. It should be so attractive that public must buy the product. There are various types of advertising like Media, Magazines. It also varies from product to product. Now the advertisement is also given on internet. Big companies endorsed Big Stars.

Till '91 Few multinational companies are working in India but after that Indian government opened gates of these companies under the Finance ministership of Dr. Manmohan Singh. India is growing economy almost every big MNC'S looking towards India.

Pepsi company launched its operation in India in '92, It was endorsed by Mr. Amir Khan and Ms. Aiswayra Rai. Most of companies endorsed established celebrities like film stars, cricketers or fresh face. Many products are endorsed by Mr. Kapil dev, Sachin Tendulkar billa billa. From inception till now hyduai company endorsed by Mr. Shah Rukh Khan.

Big companies also hired big Advertising companies to put off the burden. The Rates of advertisement which are aired in prime time are more than non prime time.

The advertisment which are used by masses are given on common magazines and channels, but products which are used by classes are given on uncommon magazines, channels and uncommon events, in Movies or IFFA awards. The anchor announces their Cold drink, Airlines and Hotel Partners. Now in Movies, In starting they display newspaper, cold drink, hotels, T.V channels billa billa.

In '89 I saw Singapore Airlines advertisement in India Today Air Hostess sat on edge of lotus pond and in pond there are lotus leafs describing their destination like Delhi, Dubai, Bangkok, Abu Dhabi, Kuwaiti, Canada, Sydney, Frankfurt. Time magazine published from Germany so there was Lufthansa advertisement, other airlines, big hotels, cars etc. Small organization printed Diaries, Clocks with name of their company and New Year calendar etc.

The marketing executive of the company also plays a vital role in selling the products, this is also a sort advertisement. They display their product in shelves in attractive manner so that customer buy the product.

Some product didn't need any advertisement. They already had a monopoly in market for e.g Lux & Pears soap, a product of Unilever. Chelpark Ink. The company and a big shop also advertisement through slide like In Patna Pvr Cinnepolies like Monte calro store, Jewerlly shop etc.

In modern Times there is little bit changed in selling the products, the company give more attention towards product like in attractive packaging, their websites and Facebook address. All companies also want to know the feed back so they are attached with call centers. The company engaged Models, Big Stars as a Brand Ambassdor for long time like Mr. Fardeen Khan of prorogue shirts, Ms. Katrina kaif of

Etihad Airlines, a National Airlines of Abu Dhabi, U.A.E. Mr. Salman Khan of Revital, Mr. Amitabh Bachan endorsed various advertisement like Novratan oil, Hajmola, Cadbury Choclates. Mr. Akshay Kumar like Honda Activa etc. Mr. Salman Khan Endorsed Thumps Up, a Product of Coca Cola with a tag line Taste the thunder.

The Advertising Agency Describing Entire Qualities of product in short (couplets), So that it eases customers to buy the product.

Company put hording and banner on various places. Companies sponsor progarme on T.V channels, in between they showed respective company advertisement.

Advertising is not limited to companies but it is wide like movies promos, Education academy like Sharda University, Frankfinn Air Hostess Academy, it was endorsed by Soha ali khan.

In every product there is a tag line like for Ghari detergent, it has a tag line *'Pehla istemal kare, phir vishwas khare'*. Eithad – Eithad Your new gateway to Abu Dhabi and the World.

Many big advertising agencies shoot product in abroad so that public will buy. Lux soap shoot in Abu Dhabi and model is Mrs. Aiswarya Rai.

If the company has a stock of product so company put an offer buy 3 get one free of same product, or on other product. T.V, Newspaper and the companies marketing executives paste the poster on their companies' shelves.

The product also be advertised in movies like Coke in Taal and Yaadein. Air India as an official airline in Pardes. Surya

Hotel in yaadien. Escorts Motorbike in Hero. Yash Chopra advertised Switzerland almost in every Movie as a tourism spot. He received many awards from there.

Airlines

Every Country has national carrier like Air India of india, Etihad airways of Abu Dhabi(The national Airline of U.A.E) , Qatar airways of Qatar, Air Mauritius of Marutius, etc.

Mr. Naresh Goyal started Jet Airways. and Suborto Roy Sahara started air Sahara. With in span of 8 to 10 years back it also flew internationally. Jet Airways put in map to Gulf Countries, Europe, U.S and Canada. For US and Canada flights jet airways make a hub in Brussels (Belgium). Later Jet Airways Accquired Sahara airlines and converted into low-cost carrier named as Jet Lite. Eithad Airways took shares from Jet airways.

Many Private Player also launched Low-cost carrier like Air Deccan by Captain Gopinath later Mr. Vijay Mallaya acquired carrier renamed King Fisher Red as Low-Cost Carrier. Mr. Mallaya also operated regular airlines named King fisher but now it ceased its operation. Mr. Ness Wadia launched Low-Cost carrier Go Air. It flew domestic sector with a two foreign destination Phuket (Thailand) and Male (Maldives). Spice jet and Indigo are also Low-Cost Carrier flew domestic and nearby abroad destination. Low-cost carrier flew its domestic destination from 1D and terminal 2 and Low-Cost Carrier to abroad from Terminal 3. Full fleged Airlines wheather flight is Domestic or foreign sector is flying from Terminal 3.

Indigo, Spice Jet and Go air are Indian based low-cost carrier.

Air Arabia launched its operation from Jaipur (India) and with in short span of time it covers entire India when I went to U.A.E I took flight from same Carrier. It is Sharjah Based Airline. In U.A.E Every Emirate has its own Airlines. Air Arabia also took intrest in South East Asia like Thailand.

In past there was no concept of low-cost carrier but when middle class and Upper middle class travelled from plane in order to save time so there are so many Low-Cost Carrier are prevailing in market.

There are 30 to 35 regular carrier are working in India like Lufthansa, KLM, British Airways, Thai airways, Emirates, Qatar Airways, Kuwait Airways, Syrian Arab Airlines, Malaysia airlines, Gulf Air, Virgin Atlantic Airlines etc. Finnair started its operation in India from 2006.

Vistara is Indian based airlines, with a tie up between Singapore Airlines and Tata Group. Tata Group has More shares. It is flying both in domestic and international sector. It is regular airline.

Many airlines changed its name with market stargy like Air India, sometimes it put International after its name, and sometime it eliminates. British Overseas Airline Company (BOAC) changed its name to British Airways. Some airlines remain its name same from its inception Like Qantas, Aeroflot etc. Mostly airline names are based on country name like Air India, Air Mauritius, Thai Airways, Qatar airways etc. And some are on different name like Cathay Pacific of Hong Kong, Etihad Airways of Abu Dhabi(The

National airline of Abu Dhabi), Aeroflot of Russia, Lufthansa of Germany etc. There are Logos along with a tag line for e.g Qantas have The Spirit of Australia, Midwest airlines –the best care in the air etc.

Low-Cost carrier (LCC) is having no classes but Regular Airlines has Class like Business or Executive, First and Economy. Eithad Airways are having Diamond, Pearl and Coral.

Every Airlines is having in-flight magazine Like magazine name of Air India is Swagat, jet lite belongs to jet lite, Selemata from Ethiopian airlines, 6E from Indigo, Enroute from Air Canada, Jet wings from Jet Airways Etc. Airline are having frequent flyer programe Like Miles & More of Lufthansa, SkyWards of Emirates, Sinbad of Oman air, Sheba Miles of Ethipion Airlines Etc.

When any Airline will launch its operation in any other country instead of launched its operation directly, Airlines give GSA to travel agencies and when agencies give green signal it will launch its operation like Minar travels are having GSA of so many Airlines like Mahan air from Iran. Minar travels fully operate Mahan air operation from city office till airport office, Now Mahan Air opened its own office. Minar Travels are having so many GSA of different airlines like Tiger airlines of Hong Kong Etc.

Bird travels are having GSA of Lufthansa. Gernal Sales Agent of Virgin Atlantic is associated to Interglobe travels. Jet airt took GSA of Gulf Air, Royal Jordian and Austrian Airlines. Dr. Subash Goyal, A Royal man and My Ideal he Wrote book "Eridication of Poverty Through tourism". STIC travels is having GSA of so many airlines like Royal Nepal Airlines, Royal Brunei, All Nippon Airlines and STIC Travels operate entire operation of SriLakan Airlines from city till the airport office.

Every Airport is having three letter code, usually city and airport code are same but sometimes airport code is different, this happened where more than one Airport like in New York there are three airport John F Kennedy (JFK), Newark (EWR), Moscow (SVO), Terminal 3 (DEL), Dubai (DXB). Airline is having two letter code like Air India, Jet airways, Emirates, American Airlines, Kuwait Airways, Singapore Airlines are AI, 9W, EK, AA, KU, SQ respectively. Logos are made on tail of aircraft with name of airlines on aircraft i.e The Maple Leaf of Air Canada, Falcon of Gulf Air, Lufthansa is having bird flying, Rising sun of Jet airways etc. Some airlines have national symbol of country as a logo.

There are Non-stop flights, Direct and Connecting Flights. If Aircraft is going towards destination and Headquater is on way Then it touched airport.

Emirates take non stop from Delhi to Dubai, with no stop.

If Mahan Air take direct flight from Delhi to Dubai from Mahan air, then only it took passenger from Imam Khomeni Airport (IKA)

If flight is going to Chicago and it is going with Gulf air then it touched Manama city, Bahrain. After some time, Passenger will take connecting flight with new Borading pass.

The First alliance took place in '97 named as "Star Alliance" Founding Member is Lufthansa and its Member are air Canada, United airlines, Thai airways etc. Air India joined Star alliance in the recent past.

The second alliance took place named as "One world, Its Members are British air, Cathay Pacific and KLM- Royal Dutch Airlines.

The Third Alliance is Sky team and their members are Delta airlines KLM –Royal Dutch Airlines, Air France, Aeroflot etc.

Many Airlines started then after ceased its operation like Archana airways, Modi Luft - A tie up between Modi Group and Lufthansa, Jagson airlines, MDLR etc. Like In India it happened in abroad Like Panam Airways.

Airline and Hotel are such an aristocratic and Glamours field. Every airline has a tie up with a hotel where the crew will stay till next flight. The entire crew members moved together to and from the airport like British Airways etc. Raddison is in tie up with SAS. The SAS crew members stayed in Radission through out globe.

Now Airline also ease ticket procedure. Before 30 years, ticket will confirm before 72 hours from the flight but today there is no need. Now there are package like Amadeus, Galieo, WordSpan etc. As soon as booking is complete and soon airline industry generates PNR code from this code we just print our ticket from everywhere or we will show ticket on our mobile when we are entering into airport. Infant has no ticket from 0-2 years, then child till 12 years only 50% and 12 and above passenger is regarded as adult.

Hartsfield- Jackson Atlanta international airport, Georgia is the busiest airport in term of passenger. Terminal 3 of Delhi is regarded as no.1 in the world. It is constructed by GMR. Emirates construct seprate terminal only for emirate Airline. In United States most of airline has own its airport.

Airbus launched A380 and took first maiden flight to India on Indira Ghandhi International Airport. Every Airlines of world ordered A380 in order to increase their Fleet. Airlines make Special class for Airbus 380. Singapore airlines unveil their class.

The Air India will also have seprate terminal in the near futre.

Visiting Cards

"Visiting Card " the important thing in the professional life whenever some officer is going to meet another officer instead of going directly in their cabins they sent their visiting cards ,in short it is brief introduction of that officer in response the later officer calls him immediately or if he is busy he ordered to serve him with great respect .My father was Chief Laision officer , I used to read his card from my childhood and I appreciated. My father is having bunch of visiting cards of other personels and they kept in folder of "Dunhill "which was presented by my maternal younger Uncle. When I was in my senior secondary, I fully aware about the importance of visiting card and I used to see cards and read them carefully. In beginning I read in absence of my father and I took permission. Mummy asked me don't see the visiting cards without permission because it is wrong morally as well as it is arranged in orderly manner because my father is a very arranged and very careful in every matter and my mother told me that my maternal grandfather and paternal grandfather were having same qualities like my father and she again repeated is the same thing if You read personal Diary or letter in absence, These are morally offense. I like visiting card of my father as well as some cards of other personnel which were given to my father by them. In 1993 when I was doing my first course of computer, so for the practice daddy gave me some card and I made different columns like names, designation, addresses of different places, telephone nos, fax etc. and next day I printed the entire list on "Lotus" and showed to my parents. From that time, I read visiting card in absence of my father. In'94 when daddy's friend's son Mr. Azeem Akbar came to our house to meet my father gave his card to us. He joined "HAMDARD" as a "MANAGER" after his M.B.A from A.M.U I liked his card because he is my ideal. With his card I will think about my card when I will print my visiting card after my studies. From that time, I will prepare my mind for M.B.A In '96 when my daddy friend Mr. Abul Hasan called him after a decade and daddy told me about him that he was in Pakistan International Airlines then In B.com I made my mind to join any good airlines after M.B.A Then I heard Azeem Bhai joined AIR INDIA so I put my stamp on my decision. In B.com I was interested in doing M.B.A with specialistion in Airline I went to skyline college but course is recognized from U.G.C. I went to Azeem bhai house in Air India colony then he gave me his new card. I like his post with logo of Air India. Then in 2002 after my B.com I joined airlines course in Sita Academy with an aim to join any good airlines especially British Airways. In same year I visited to exibition at Pragati Madan ,I reached counter of visting card then I took one card as a sample with a thought to print my card in coming months after completing my airlines course .but this dream of mine is still a dream but I didn't got a job in any airlines or even travel agency.In 2009 I went to dubai and I joined Royal city contracting as a accounts officer as well as I had look certain HR activities. My two colleagues Mr. Nisar

Ahmed and Mr. Basit joined the company with me as an interior manager and costing manager resp. so my chairman orderd my immediate boss to print cards for Mr. Nisar and Mr. Basit then I thought about my card but he didn't order about my card. I felt so bad because I expected my card in this company.

Unknown Lane

I Walk on my residence lane for about 43 years but uptil now I gave my introduction on every morning when I opened my door. When I meet person who met with me several times or for the first time, I saw various questions in their both eyes and in mind. Several times they asked me and who are mature they kept in their minds. Most of them asked me Do you recognized me, I am having answer that I am orthopedic patient not mentally. Often, I avoided parties but some parties are important. From there I came in bad mood and sometime happy. But before it's a very difficult task for me should I attend parties or not.

Some person who likes me but also, they don't want to spent a with me. They asked me some repeatedly questions with me and excuse me I am just coming. I don't understand why people behave me like this.

Rampur is small town so everybody met very oftenly. But nobody accepted me in normal way. I just want to find company in my friend, my maternal uncle friend and paternal uncle's friend but they avoided me, only I stood for little time and moved to another group.

In my residence lane nobody talks me, everybody neglected me in bad manner so near about everyday I came to my home in aggressive mood. I don't have potential to retaliate them so I asked my parents what I will do ,Even my Cousin neglected me.

I finished my studies in 2002 so from that time till now I am waiting for any good opportunity but it didn't came in my way.

Everybody thought I am mentally weak so nobody gave me offer even in my city as well in Delhi . I am Physically challenged but I have certain other qualities i.e. I am honest, devotee to my work, dedicated etc no body like this on the contrary if a person is dishonest but he is physically fit so everyone gave him a job.

My parents gave proposal for me to good families even they praises me as well as my family but they rejected me on the basis of my Physically weakness. Somebody refused in sugarcoated way and other in bad way. On my first proposal, She (my paternal aunty) said about me in such way my mother wept all the way as well as my daddy told my mother his friend also rejected.

So in My narrow lane as well as city is concerned I didn't have any acquaintance. Nobody came to me only for meeting with me . In my lane only Mosque welcome me in a good manner but there also mostly all of them saw me in systrac way. In a nutshell all people avoided me in one way or other So How I will spent my life?

According to me everybody thinks that I am curse to society and If I will go, I will having infect from this disease. After completing my studies we also thought I will achieve some height and I will on same train but neither I catch the same train nor somebody gave his hand to pull me up. From outside I am thinking how is the train and passengers I am only passenger waiting for my train and days ,months and year Passed speedly I am going towards Grave.

The known poet Bashir badr poet said but it is said on me

KOI HATH BHI NA MILEGAYGA JO GALEE MILE GAYE TAPAK SE,

YEAH NAYE MAJIS LOG HAIN YAHAN SE FASLA SE MILA KARO.

I went to airport to receive and see off my sister, my cousin or I am going somewhere, the crowd didn't criticize on me. I thought they accompany for a short time or they are classy crowd.

Criticism is easy task but who will face it is a difficult task. Every day I woke up with a new hope but end of day I am tired. When I went to school I spent my school hours with so much difficulty.

On the other side When I came in house I felt relaxed , My parents asked me is everything is alright, I said Yes but when I said yes some small incident happened and when I wept there is something wrong but my parents welcome and boost my morale. My parents are always worried for me. They are dignified personas. The room, varenda and my swing are witness of my weeping , My swing which my father gifted to my sister and me in '92. The swing is witness of my failures. They heard and absorb in it like my parents. But I admired every corner of my house, they reply me in their own way. From our Childhood till today house is witness of our activities, my parents and younger sister cooperated me side by side. I am unable to do some work like to wear school uniform, My father cooperates me, my little sister polished my shoes and my Mummy packed my lunch with lot of tears in her eyes. She asked her collegue I sent him in school............. But How he will spend the entire day. While my father is helping me in wearing my uniform he told me how you will knot a tie and wearing a coat , you put only one button while sitting you also opened that button also. He put a hanky in upper pocket in a stylish way. My father moved a high society and his nature to picked a good things from everywhere.

When I am interested in aviation sector I read so many airliners and travel agents but I like Mr. Subash Goyal who is owner of Stic Travles. His dressing is also up to the mark. He started his travels in '74.

In my childhood when my parents took opinion from different doctors they told he will study and other activities but he will be slow. So, this happened, Now my classmates, my elder and younger cousin is spending a normal life. I just asked with my parents when I will marry and spend a normal life, they also don't know but they said you will also be soon in this category.

My brother in law is also be gentle person, he is thinking for me .He called me and took me to several places for e.g in a travel agency ...billa billa. Alas I received a negative response because I don't have a motorbike.

Whenever we met our classmates, he asked me in a criticized way what are you doing and are you married or not. When my marriage was going on, they and other person said different question publicly.

We are completely comfortable in GOD wish but when person asked various question and laugh on me so I wept and doing abnormal activities.

There is silver lining even after some days but I didn't see for about 30 years.

As far as my professional life is concerned many proposals were in the pipeline but not even a single proposal is implemented but I hope a recent proposal will be complete .

I took birth in this Unknown Lane and everyday passed through dawn and dusk, I am going towards my grave where we will spend endless life. No one want to share a cup of tea with me except a few person esp. my parents.

Isolation

The person who is leading a isolated life is in very bad phase. The larger section of society gave isolation who is having some type of drawbacks. Person is doing struggle inside him in addition to negligence of society. The qualities of isolated person is invisible overcome by his any type of weakness. The isolated person creates own way for spending his/her life but it's very difficult.

From '89 I spent an isolated life before this I really didn't felt isolated . When children called my cousin to play cricket and I left alone in house . In '88 When I took admission in Green Wood I requested to my principal that I will deliver speech on 15th Aug. then she rejected me . When my elder cousin sent my younger cousin by cycle and stopped me, It hit my sentiments. There were several matters like this. My mummy was in college and my father was also busy in business. I created my own small world. I didn't attended all marriages and parties. Some functions are very important but when I returned with lot of burden on my mind and it took one or two days in coming to normal atmosphere. Everybody ignore me . In gatherings I alone walked here and there , so I enjoyed with delicious food. Now I am 48 years old, I am not having any friend as well as I don't have any companion. As the year passed I got more mature I suggested for me that Isolation is best for me and I follow policy of Escapism from society. In my house I talked very much in order to compensate. In one reception of my cousin, I humiliated by one classmate in front of 10 classmates. He attacked on my personal issues , till that moment my marriage life was going on.

I read Newspaper, India Today etc. In India Today of Jan '89 I read interview of Industrialist Manu Chabria who owns a shop in Mumbai to big building of JUMBO ELECTRONICS in Dubai. He started company on 1st jan. 1974 with help of four Arabian partners. He also acquired many sick units. When I saw airlines advertisement in news paper or in magazine , I got thrilled . I read TIMES of INDIA in interest to saw airlines advertisement and their schedule from and to Delhi . In Times of India I read mostly business section and page3 news. Whenever I went to airport I took schedules of airlines from airport office like GULF AIR , UZBEKISTAN AIRLINES etc. I also read TRAV TALK which is fortnightly travel magazine. In India Today I also read entire story of Naresh Goyal of JET AIRWAYS when he acquired SAHARA AIRLINES and turned into low cost carrier JET LITE. I thought to start my own travels or to acquire sick travel agency. I started to take information on this and I discussed with my SITA academy Principal but this also turned in negative direction. In this small world which I created around me I don't want to disturb by anybody.

In '90 one teacher didn't take interest although he is my relative. He ignore me because I didn't take tution from him. He took three periods . In his period I am sitting ideal . I am unable to write notes. In this way my valuable years were wasted slowly. I completed my education with a gap of 5 yreas and I lost 23 years professionally. If I was in some good airlines or in reputed travel agency I got one or two promotion.

Till today I didn't fill that gap. In 2002 I thought the difficult time was over. When I came into practical world I faced more difficult time than before till today. When my maternal grand ma left this world in '02 I didn't achieved anything , I think she was a lucky mascot for me.

In 1993 Satellite channel came into market and we took intrest in many new programme on ZEE tv and other channels . The programme are Hum Honge Kamyab on ZEE. Young Trunks on CNBC anchored by Miss Sheen Bhan. I also watched interviews of Adi Godrej, Vijay Path Singhnia, Vijay Mallaya, Naresh Goyal , Subhash Goyal etc. I was regular viewer of Musafir Hoon Yaron on Star plus hosted by Miss Deepti Bhatnagar . In 1995 I also saw DASTAN serial , It was story of successful businessman . The entire serial was shooted in Dubai . Parmeet Sethi played a central role. I thought it was biopic of Manu Chabria . I like Parnoy Roy who gave a programme THE WORLD THIS WEEK in 1990, He also gave election analysis aired on Doordarshan and latestly I admired the style of Rajdeep Sardesai. I watched meaningful movies ,Pakistani dramas, listening songs and ghazals .

From recent past laptop also plays a vital role in my life till now. On this only I started writing and I received good comments . My Mummy encouraged me what you have in our mind put it down on paper. She is also a good writer,

Her one book was published "APNA HI GRAMAN BHUL GAYE."

I am spending a retirement life . I didn't statisfy with anything because I am not leading normal life. My parents are going towards old age and they are thinking about me how he will spend life after us. Along with our parents my sister and her husband thought about me.

I am totally flopped in every walk of life whether it is Professionally ,Personally and Socially. Every body maintained a distance from me . They don't want to interact me. I called everybody but nobody called me. Now I am spending two lives one which is going in reality and one in my mind If I am like others then how I spend my life. Whenever I want to swim my weakness became hurdle. My past affected my present and future both. Everyone tried to statisfy me with their talks.

FURSAT AGAR MILE TO MUJHE PAD KAR DEKHAYE

MUJEAY (Title) ZINDIGI PE MUKAMAL KITAB HOON